MW01124198

Light and Shadow

TRUTH AND REALITY

Jan Douglas Bish

Copyright © 2006 by Jan Douglas Bish

ISBN 0-7414-3521-7

Cover Art by Jan Douglas Bish

Cover Design by Jan Douglas Bish

"You Needed Me" by Ann Murray © 1990 Cema

Published by:
INFI∞ITY
PUBLISHING.COM
1094 New DeHaven Street, Suite 100
West Conshohocken, PA 19428-2713
Info@buybooksontheweb.com
www.buybooksontheweb.com
Toll-free (877) BUY BOOK
Local Phone (610) 941-9999
Fax (610) 941-9959

Printed in the United States of America

Printed on Recycled Paper

Published November 2006

Other Published books by Jan Bish:

A New Revelation of Israel

Trump Your Trouble

So This is the Garden of Eden

Bequeath the Wind

An Ian Bishop Adventure

Introduction

Can you imagine what the Spirit Realm is like where God lives? Do you know where it is and how to get there? Are you able to visualize what it would be like to live in a world of many levels, dimensions and layers? Just imagine a place of beautiful mountains, lush valleys and vast oceans. You should be able to conceive of all these things because this is where you live.

Now, I want you to step into another dimension. This dimension will be right on the other side of the third, fourth and fifth dimensions, one you did not think existed, or if you knew of this place, you thought that it was way off beyond the stars and planets somewhere, in a far off galaxy.

This is the Realm of God.

Actually we might even visit as many as seven more dimensions. You have known of the three dimensions in this physical world already, because you can see them with your physical eyes.

You can not see the fourth dimension, but you know of it.

The fourth dimension is time, and you are traveling through that dimension even as you read this book.

In the Spirit Realm of God you will experience a world without time and gravity, a world traveling at the speed of Light. You will find a place without tears or sorrow, a world filled with peace. See the prism of light and color, listen to the Master of the universe play His symphony of strings.

This will be a journey through my life, of actual experience with the Spirit Realm, into Bible Truth, and beyond. We will even travel through Quantum Physics to the place where God lives, and discover how you too, can be more in touch with God's Spirit and the spirit within.

This is not Science Fiction or "Pie in the Sky".

We will begin in this natural realm, and you will see how we interact with the Spirit Realm of God.

What He has revealed to me, He will reveal to your understanding. You will see and understand the slow progression through my life, from birth to rebirth and beyond.

We will also visit the lowest spiritual realm, into that dimension where Satan (Lucifer) lives with his demonic hosts. And, we will clearly see his influence in this world and the way he roams the earth seeking whom he may devour from that fifth dimension.

However, I want you to keep in mind that there are more of us, than there is of them. Only one third of the angels fell with Satan. Two thirds are on your side!

We will travel in the fourth dimension, back in time to the Biblical Truth of "In the beginning," and ascertain the true meaning of Spiritual Warfare, that plagues us even today.

And finally we will travel to the pinnacle of infinity. There we will see the truth of General Relativity and Quantum Mechanics. In that realm of thought you will see that the physical realm is surrounded by seven different dimensions of parallel worlds. Those parallel worlds are without time as we know it. It is a place that defies gravity. Yet, they are our neighbors, the Spirit Realm of God.

ক

Science may not yet, be able to totally prove Quantum Physics String Theory, "The Theory of Everything," but this is the direction and the path of the quantum physicist of today.

It has always required a Leap of Faith to reach God.

And, that seems to be the way God likes it. This new concept, however has lead us to a new understanding of God's Creation. Beyond Quantum Physics and Relativity is the place where God rules from, and lives.

ক

We will be looking at Truth as looking into the face of a diamond with many facets. We will learn how to effectively use our **imaginations** to see into the Spiritual Realm. Being able to "IMAGE" something is a good thing. Without VISION, God's people perish. Physicists have come to understand that what they thought were different theories, actually have been the same theory as seen from different directions or perspectives.

Take each life experience, and each revelation and every Scripture in this book and you will be able to put all these pieces together like a jig saw puzzle and you too will see and understand world history, the spiritual realm, the universe and eternity.

ক

Lately, I have been questioning God. "What am I to do with all this information from You and my life experiences? "

And God said, "**Share it!**"

He instructed me to start at the beginning, because you can not understand the future until you understand the past. My life has mostly been Light and Shadow.

ॐ

WE WILL BEGIN IN THIS NATURAL REALM:

I was more than just a little reluctant to enter this world.

I didn't know what to expect.

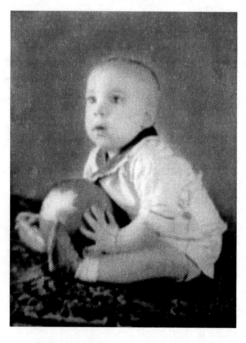

MASTER JAN DOUGLAS BISH

Not knowing what lays around the next corner comes with a certain amount of trepidation.

Being birthed can be a very harrowing experience. You might know what I mean. Since you are reading this story. You too, probably came into this world the same way that I did. We are birthed through pressure, under gravity and thrust into time.

I made my dramatic grand entrance, not even with a whimper.

However, I was kicking and screaming all the way.

Life in this realm is a traumatic encounter.

My earliest recollection was arriving at my new home in Meadville, Pennsylvania, from the hospital, as a new born. I clearly and distastefully remember little old ladies pinching my cheeks and baby talking to me. I really did not like that. I still don't like being "talked down to."

And, the "little old ladies" probably were not so little, or all that old.

That my friends, is all **relative** to your situation.

Didn't Einstein have a theory on that, called: "Relativity?" (Just kidding with you.)

૱

Speaking of relatives, we didn't have a lot to say about that, as far as choosing our parents. God and His infinite wisdom had that all figured out before we were sent into this world.

There does seem to be some things planted within our inner core, that is from our parents and dictates some of who we are.

I also believe that ultimately we turn out to be the sum total of our own experiences.

FAITH AND HOPE

Faith is a substance that we bring over from the other side and is a part of our spirit.

Without FAITH we would not have the substance of things hoped for in our lives.

Without HOPE, we would be lost in a hostile world. These are spiritual elements that help us survive in this environment.

INTRUCTION MANUAL

There are a lot of people in this world that do not exercise their spirit. You know the Bible does say that physical exercise is good, but spiritual exercise can profit you in this world and the one to come.

We are also given Spiritual tools to build our life with a firm foundation. Those tools are: The Word of God. He created all that is, by the power of His Word. We are created in the image and likeness of God.

Therefore we should be speaking positive things into existence with His Word.

We are also a Trinity; spirit, soul and body.

God told me "**Don't ever let anyone tell you that My Word does not work.**" And, then He said, "**You work My Word.**" You can use God's Word as Spiritual Tools to create your physical realities.

You did come into this world with an instruction manual. Some parents don't bother to read it. And, some of you would rather stumble around in the dark and find your own way.

There are a lot of "lost people" in this world that can not find their own way.

Here's hoping that through this book, some of you will find your way back to the Truth and a new reality for your physical lives.

You see TRUTH never changes.

The physical realm (your reality) is always in a state of flux. I was birthed into this world of so-called reality. I say, so-called because the dimension of Spiritual Truth is ever-lasting, a world without end.

As for now, I see dimly as looking through a fog on to deeper truths, because I live in the shadow of Spiritual Light and Truth.

That however does not mean that we will not be able to see what lays ahead. You may be at an intersection in your life, trying to choose which road to follow, but the fog is so thick, it is difficult to see which road looks the best. You may have to take the hand of a friend. A Friend that has been here before and allow Him to guide you down the right path. What a Friend we have in Jesus.

"SUMMER DAY "by Jan Douglas Bish, An early work in Crayon!

In Elementary School, I remember almost dying at least three times. Well, that's the way I felt.

Once I fell down a hill and had the breath knocked out of me. To a small child, that feels like you are dying because you can not breathe.

On another occasion I was also alone, and walking across the school yard. I got choked up for no reason, that I could understand and could not get enough air to breathe. That has happened to me several times. I have suffered with the fear of choking to death ever since.

There was another time when I jumped into the deep end of a swimming pool, before I knew how to swim. I saw the other kids swimming and it didn't look that hard.

If it wasn't for the life guard that pulled me out, I would have drowned.

That was the first time I jumped in over my head, but not the last. I seem to have a knack for getting in over my head.

I recall a time when I only wished that I was dead. I saw a big bully waiting to beat me up, outside the gate of this house. (pictured below) My childhood home.

Home on 72nd. Street near Seat Pleasant, Md.

Much of what I have shared with you as well as the things I am about to reveal, I have just kept to myself. I have always been a very private person.

⚬

As a kid, I always lived in my own private little world and didn't let anyone inside.

I was always living in fear as a youth. I was afraid that when I grew up that I would be poor. From the time that I was in elementary school I knew that I wanted to be an artist or be on the stage. I knew that would be just about impossible so I was anxious for my future. Sometimes I even wondered if I would live that long.

Pictured above is Jan and his mother,
On the back of this photograph his mother wrote;
"If you look real close you will see someone who really likes to play with string." You don't suppose that I was interested in String Theory way back then do you?

I was afraid of the bullies that didn't like me. At times, I was even terrified of my father. I felt like I was under attack from a very early age, as though I was in a battle for my life.

Most of my fear, I know NOW was a lie that came straight out of Hell. (That fifth spiritual dimension where Lucifer lives with his evil spirits)

You see, now I understand that "fear" is the opposite force of "faith". Where there is FAITH, faith will repel fear. I have learned how to LIVE BY FAITH.

᷉

"Opposing forces" is another principle of Quantum Physics (String Theory).

"When you open the door to fear, faith will fly out the window."

I did have a few diversions along the way...

While in Elementary School.

I remember once I lined up, out on the playground with a bunch of other boys to kiss the best looking girl in school. (and she knew it!) The line, was her idea. The recess bell rang right before it was my turn.

Talk about disappointing!

(*In later years I saw that girl again. She was wearing an old worn out dress and had two little kids pulling at her apron strings and another one in her arms. Not so cute any more, I thought.*)

I was not the sharpest tool in the tool shed, but I did well with the things that held my interest.

There was one time I recall, not my brightest moment, when I played hooky from school. I didn't go far. There was a hill that over-looked the playground. I skipped a class that I did not like and took my bagged lunch up the hill. I think that I wanted to be a king of all that I surveyed, if only for a moment.

I wanted to be **in charge** of my own life.

(*We all want control over our own life.*)

The problem was; I was not in-charge. The gym teacher saw me on the top of that hill and I got in trouble.

It was much later in my life that I discovered that we are

never really **in-charge.** Some of us just think that we are!

We are always under authority. No matter how hard we fight against it, that authority is always there.

We were created to have a free will, and free choice, but if we do not do what is right, we get ourselves in trouble just like that day on top of the playground hill.

There was a small Baptist Church within walking distance of the house where I grew up. However, as a family, we attended Seat Pleasant Methodist Church, near the Washington, D.C. line, every Sunday.

My mother taught Sunday School and my father was the Church Treasurer.

I really think the reason that my dad wanted to be treasurer was because he got to go through all the coins. He collected coins in blue books according to their amount and the year minted.

I liked Sunday School, but I had trouble making it all the way through church. I had to sit still and be quiet.

I was never very good with either one of those attributes.

I still have trouble sitting still for too long at a time and even God knows that the only time I am quiet is at three o'clock in the morning. When Jesus was out in the middle of the Sea of Galilee and said "**Peace, be still**". I think He was talking to me as well as to Simon Peter.

I have always needed the peace of God in my life and I definitely need to be still. You know there is a scripture that says;

"Be still and know that I am God."

The reason I mentioned three o'clock in the morning is because God likes to wake me up to talk with me then.

I finally got tired of that, and asked Him;

"Why do you wake me up at three in the morning?"

He said; "Because that's the only time you are quiet."

So I would recommend that if you don't like being woke up in the early morning hours that you set aside some "quiet time" during the day.

❧

The reason that God had kids: It was an extension of His love and for fellowship. He desires to have fellowship with you. It does not matter to God, if that time is three am or three pm, because there is no time in the spiritual realm.

The time might matter to you, though.

That is why a day is as a thousand years to God.

JAN AND HIS OLDER SISTER, ZILLA ANN

My older sister was my only sister, and she was good at it! We did not have much in common because of the age difference, but she would take me with her sometimes, when she went to Seneca Lake or to Great Falls. The rest of the time I felt like she was" too Bossy." There was one time that she ordered me to dry dishes and

I didn't want to.

I threw something, I don't remember what, but it did go through the kitchen window. Whoops!

(My sister and I get along much better now that I have matured and we have more things in common.)

I lived a fantasy. I was always playing a role, like I was in a movie. I made up the script as I went along, but the cameras were always rolling. That was my way of dealing with the reality of life as I knew it. I didn't really like the real world much.

My mother loved me, but she was always at work during the day in a department store (7th floor dry goods) in downtown Washington, D.C.

My father was a Proof Reader at the Government Printing Office in D.C. He was a day sleeper (so I had to be <u>very</u> quiet). He worked at night. I never was a quiet kind of guy. One time I was playing down in the basement of our house. He was two floors above me in his bedroom.

What I didn't realize was that there was a furnace vent right where I was playing, and it went straight into his room beside his bed.

Whoops, again!

Maybe he was trying to get even with me for waking him up (as a kid, that's what I thought).

Then again, he probably was just not happy with himself and took it out on me and maybe he was just tired. Or, maybe all of the above.

He required that I leave my school home work papers on the kitchen table at night before I went to bed.

When I got up every morning, I had to face all my school work covered with red penciled corrections.

I soon learned all the proof reader's terms and symbols, but that was ALL I learned from that experience. Then, I had to do my home work again, before school.

I only had one or two friends and I couldn't play with them most of the time because I had chores to do. Room to clean, a big double yard to mow with a push mower, etc. I can say that I truly learned a work ethic at an early age.

Later, I would tell my children how I walked to school on those cold winter mornings...in the snow...up hill...Both ways...Over 2 miles!

They would respond by saying "Oh, no!

Not that story again."

Well, that's a lot for little legs.

I remember one warm summer evening. I went for a walk by myself and ended up on the steps of that Baptist Church. I heard the singing and saw a sign that said; "Revival". I didn't know what Revival meant but I did understand music. I went down front in that little church and accepted Jesus that evening to the refrain; "Just as I am". But, as far as I could tell, that was it. Nothing apparently changed in the physical realm, but now that I look back at that evening the angels must have rejoiced because something happened in the spiritual realm that was going to eventually change my physical realities and touch many other lives.

Meanwhile I just continued to live my day to day existence, doing my own thing. I thought about God every now and then, but did not yield to Godly principles. I did the wrong things and got into trouble the same as before, and only turned to God when I was really in trouble. I even ran away from home once. The police caught me, and my father had me locked up for three months (reform school) to "put the fear of God in me". Of course that didn't do any good. It just made me even more upset with my father.

In Junior High School, I started to come into my own. I taught myself to play the guitar. I loved to sing.

Actually I loved all the creative arts. (not knowing that it would shape my life and future)

I formed a musical group, a trio. We called ourselves "The Harmony Boys" and we played at "Openings," Dances and local Washington, D.C. TV and Radio. Why, I even played a "Harmony" guitar.

Later in life, I heard that the boy that played the accordion in my musical group "The Harmony Boys," became a fireman in D.C. and retired. The other boy who played an electric harmonica, had died of a drug overdose before he finished high school.

"THE HARMONY BOYS"
David Reynolds, Jan Bish and Ken Selby

I always got straight A's in Art, Music and Theater, but then again, so did everyone else that showed up for class. So that really did not matter. I didn't get the credit I thought I deserved for the A's that I had received.

The "important things," the core subjects were not the things I was interested in and I only did what was necessary and required to get by.

❧

High School was not too different from Jr. High, except my parents divorced (which I thought was partially my fault) because I did not get along well with my father. Later I found out that he was not a faithful husband and it really was not my fault.

I did learn from that and vowed to myself that I would

NEVER be unfaithful. I experienced the pain and the consequences from what he had done, and I learned from his experience that time.

My father married the woman that he fell in love with, at his office. It turned out that he was not faithful to his new wife either.

See the brand new "Nash" in the driveway!

My mother moved out of our beautiful new house
in Cheverly, Maryland.

With money my father had given my mom, she bought a new Prairie Schooner House Trailer (45 feet long) with two bedrooms for her and me. I found the trailer house very interesting. It even had a front screened-in porch that dropped down over the hitch.

Prairie Schooner was the original company that made **covered wagons** in the old west.

Don't look at me that way! No, I am not THAT old.

ॐ

When I retired, I bought a Prairie Schooner Travel Trailer. They are making them different now. Four Slide Outs, Island Kitchen, Fireplace, Built-in Flat Screen Tvs and theater sound systems, Etc.

Young Love, True Love,
came my way in High School.

Oh, I had felt "puppy love" before but never anything like this! Her name was Betty Lou. The first time I saw her was all the way across a crowded restaurant. **She took my breath away.** I knew that I was ready for the old "Ball and Chain" when I met her. I was a prisoner of L O V E.

I said to my best friend sitting beside me; "Who is that beautiful girl over there?" He said "You can ask her brother. He's sitting across the table from you."

I did just that, and a whole new chapter in my life had begun.

She was 12 years old (soon to be 13) and I was 16. At first I remember just driving around the block, where she lived, singing with the song on the radio, "On the Street Where You Live". I was driving my mother's 54 Chevy. At first I didn't have enough nerve to stop, park and walk up the sidewalk to her front door. I even feared that she might be looking out the window.

After my third trip over to her house, I finally went up to her door and knocked. She opened the door and from then on, we were a matched set.

You would see us at the Sock Hops in the school gym, at the ice cream shop, going out for Pizza, or slow dancing to the romantic strains of "Love me Tender" on the old 45s in the "Ruckus Room" of her folks house. But, you would never see us apart.

After high school I went on active duty with the U.S. Marines. I was already in the U.S.M.C. Reserves while attending high school. My duty station was to be Camp Lejeune, N.C.

I could not bear the thought of being without her so I asked her to marry me.

Her parents had to approve because she was not yet 16 years old. Her mother even paid for our honeymoon to Virginia Beach, Virginia. On the first day, Betty Lou got so sunburned, I could not touch her (literally).We were both virgins.

Betty also had another problem, that I understand was taken care of in later years by surgery. Our marriage was never consummated but I loved her deeply. I took her to North Carolina with me and I applied for base housing. The housing was assigned and we moved in. It came with furniture and appliances. Not much to look at, and when you turned out the lights, the roaches came out to play, but it was our first home together. A home filled with love, not lust. "TOGETHER" being the key word.

She was to continue her high school education on base.

Her mother came down to North Carolina while I was at work one day and took Betty back to Maryland.

Betty was after all, a very young lady and a "momma's girl". I mean that in the nicest way. I still love that girl. When I got home from work I expected to find Betty, a kiss and a hug waiting for me. All I found was a note on my kitchen table and a very empty house. I was alone and devastated.

I applied for emergency leave the very next morning, from

the Marines. I followed them back to Maryland from North Carolina, but Betty Lou's mother would not let me see her.

I had to return to base, and I had to face the fact that Betty's mother was going to have the marriage **Annulled.**

(*Like it had never taken place, like we never made a commitment or had said: Till death do us part.*)

Maybe I should have exerted myself more than I did at the time, but I have always had a problem with pushing people to do things that they did not want to do. Sometimes I think that I should have just pushed my way in and demanded my rights as her husband, but I was young also and not wise to the ways of this world.

I would never have forced Betty to do anything that she apparently, did not want.

My song became "I don't have Anything, Since I don't have You."

I remembered a song I had once sung on the television in D.C.
"Oh Yes, I'm The Great Pretender".

They say if you don't sing the Gospel, you'll sing the Blues!

Was I supposed to pretend that I didn't love her any more?

I went through the rest of my service days as if in a trance, only going through the motions of life, but feeling dead inside. You will either totally relate to this or not understand at all. How could I get to this point in my life and think I had experienced EVERYTHING? I felt like, if I died that day, I would not have missed a single thing and I wasn't even twenty years old.

After my Honorable Discharge, I decided to go to school at Roberts Wesleyan College in North Chili, N.Y. I figured that I would major in psychology, maybe teach high school students. I needed answers to life's questions. It didn't take me long to realize that psychology had more questions than answers. I was told to read the book; "I'm OK, Your OK". I understood the title so I figured I didn't need to read the book. What can I say? It was a great title!

Psychology was suppose to help you understand yourself, and if you understood yourself, you would understand others better. I also read books like "The Power of Positive Thinking".

All of this was good, but not complete. I had even more questions and there did not seem to be answers, or if there were answers, the answers came with more questions.

While I was going to college, I worked an eight hour midnight shift as a Die Mounter at St Joe Paper Company in Rochester, N.Y.. I took morning classes, did my home work during lunch and then went to work. That left no time for any social life, but I wasn't feeling real social anyway.

I had room and board at a house across from school on Orchard Street. One morning I woke up with snow on the foot of my bed. The snow had blown in through unseen cracks around the closed window. I figured that it was time for me to "blow" as well, to a warmer clime.

I started looking for a St. Joe Paper Company as far south as possible. I found one in Florida and one in Houston, Texas. Houston was a little further south so I transferred my job to Houston.

I asked my mother, who was living alone in Pennsylvania at the time, if she wanted to go to Houston with me?

She said; "They don't have trees down there."

I said "Sure they do, Mom".

So, she came down south with me and we settled in Texas.

My love of art was deep within, demanding to be loosed. It was as though God had placed that interest within me, so I began to pursue it. I found the Regal School of Art in Houston, and graduated from their two year program.

I began to work commercially, but soon discovered that commercial art was too confining. I found myself doing things to satisfy others, instead of doing my work the way I wanted to do it.

Later in my art career I was to discover that although I *chose* art,

I began to feel that art had really CHOSEN ME.

An Original Painting by Jan Douglas Bish

**"IF IT WASN'T FOR THE LIGHT HOUSE,
WHERE WOULD THIS SHIP BE?"**

My art was like a compulsive calling on my life. I became enveloped by it.

Also about this same time I was in another music group, kind of like the Kingston Trio. We did all of their songs on local Houston TV. I still played the guitar and sang.

JAN and JOYCE

The song that I was singing then, was "The Second Time Around"

Love really was better the second time around for me.

Her name was Joyce. She was to be the mother of my children. We had a lot of mutual friends through a Methodist Youth Group, M.Y.F. I first saw her picture in the high school year book and told one of my friends, that I wanted a date with her. So, here we go, our friends fixed us up on a "Blind Date".

I picked Joyce up in my little red and white convertible sports car. It was a beautiful day. I had the top down and parked in the parking lot beside the Old Majestic Theater in downtown Houston.

After the movie. I noticed that it looked like rain, so after seating Joyce in my car, I reached back to manually pull the top up. Then I realized, too late that it had been raining while we were at the movie.

The folds of the top were full of water and it was as though I had thrown a bucket of water over Joyce's head. You can see that I made a big impression on her, on our very first date.

I had already made a date for Joyce's high school prom with a friend of hers, even though I was four to five years older. Joyce already had a date for her senior prom, but that was the last date we had with anyone else. We were married a few months later. We were together for eighteen years.

Our first born came along right after our first wedding anniversary. Her name was Valarie. She was so good, we had to wake her, for her two am feeding. The doctor said; "Let her sleep." So, we did!

I was just finishing art school and was working in Commercial Art, Newspaper Advertising and Sales. We were bored and wanted something more in our lives, so we sold our house, bought a small travel trailer and headed for California to find our fame and fortune.

I got a job with the Santa Barbara News Press and started painting in my spare time. I sold my art work along Cabrillo Blvd. next to the beach on weekends. It wasn't long before my art income surpassed my payroll check. Joyce encouraged me to be a full time artist.

I quit my "real job" to become an artist and started doing art shows all over the country. Joyce and I traveled Europe searching for subject matter to paint. I traveled the U.S. and

Canada doing the art circuit for many years. That's kind of like a performer doing "one night stands." We had a beautiful home in the hills of Santa Barbara, overlooking the city, and the Channel Islands in the Pacific Ocean.

In the summer, our whole family would travel together in our motor home.

I would do "back to back" art shows in different parts of the country. Set up shows, tear down shows and hopefully make a few sales in between.

Being a professional artist was not easy and at times it seemed like feast or famine. At times, it was!

We had three beautiful daughters.

One time a school teacher asked my daughter, Valarie, what I did for a living. She replied; "He paints old houses and old boats". The school teacher listed me as a house painter on her school information forms.

Many years had passed. We moved to New Braunfels, Texas and opened Bish Art Gallery. I had ordered some of my art prints from one of my publishers, for our gallery. When the package arrived from California, I discovered that the publisher had made a mistake. They had included an art print by some other artist, of a Jewish Rabbi.

What was I going to do with that?

It would cost me money to return it, so I kept it. We framed it and put it in our front gallery window. Now that was foolish, wasn't it? A Jewish Rabbi in a German town!

Who would buy such a thing? I had just put the framed Rabbi in the window and it attracted a man, in off the street. He was a Bible Scholar, Teacher and Christian Film Producer. He bought the "Rabbi" art print for his office and fell in love with my original art work.

The Bible Scholar told me that he was working on a manuscript and he wanted me to illustrate his new book. He also said that if I went to Israel with him that he would pay my way. Now I didn't really have any interest in Israel. It was nothing more than a desert wilderness, right?

That was like my mother saying: "There are no trees in Texas."

I decided that I would go to Israel. It was after all, a free trip to the other side of the world.

JAN WORKING ON A PAINTING FROM ISRAEL

THE ADVENTURE

While in Israel, I began searching for subject matter that would be of interest for my new friend's book.

We went to the official flag maker in Jerusalem and I bought an Israeli flag with the Star of David as a souvenir of my trip.

After returning home I began working on this new series of paintings. My friend's book never came to fruition, but an original series of paintings entitled; "A Tour of Israel" came into being.

Something very unusual started happening.

I would do a painting from the subject matter that I found in Israel and after the painting was finished, the meaning and significance of that work would come to me through my thinking, and I knew as the artist that I did not have any of that in mind while doing the painting.

Like so many people, I still wanted to feel like I controlled my own life.

That feeling came back to me all the way from elementary school. Well, I knew that I did not have much control over anything else in my life, but I at least knew that I could control my art work.

I could create original works of art. That gave me a feeling of accomplishment. The more I allowed the Lord to work through my paintings, the less control I seemed to have. However, that did take a lot of pressure off my shoulders and also taught me more about living by faith. God began to show me how His Spirit works in the world today, through my own paintings.

Every painting became a new lesson. Life lessons, on how the spiritual realm and the physical mesh and work together. I could see how the spiritual realm can cross over into this physical dimension using our own spirit as a conduit.

I had always wanted to do the kind of paintings that had story form, flowing from within, and now I could see that happening. But it was a little daunting, because I knew it was not me doing that. At this same time, I was working in my art studio, located in the basement area of our art gallery.

Joyce came into my studio and said; "Jan, you have to come up stairs to the gallery. There is a woman sitting on the floor crying in front of the paintings you have been working on, from Israel."

I came into the gallery and found out that the lady had just returned from Israel. She was on her way through town, to her home in Lubbock, Texas. Due to a flood she was temporarily stranded in New Braunfels. She had just come in off the street, guided by God's Spirit.

When I found out that she was from Lubbock, I said; "I have an art showing scheduled in Lubbock this next week". So she told me she would come see me at the art showing in Lubbock, Texas.

The lady who had just come from Israel did show up at my art showing the following week. She wanted me to go to a Bible Study with her and her husband.

I said "No, The show won't close till nine pm."

"It's okay, if we get there late." She said.

I told her; "I am in my Motor Home and don't want to move it, and didn't know where the Bible Study house is".

"My husband and I will pick you up."

I replied to that, "After the show is over, I will be tired, and hungry."

She said; "We will go out to eat together afterwards."

What is a man to do? She answered every excuse I could come up with. When God wants you to be someplace, God will see to it that you are there. So I ignored the other "whisperings" in my ear and said; "Yes. "

That evening was one of the most astounding evenings of my life!

We arrived late. The Bible Study was just about over. As we walked in the door, I was facing the man that was conducting the study. I could sense that something was about to happen. We both did a double take of each other but this man did not know me, nor did I know him. Matter of fact I knew no one in that room except the lady I had just met by chance in my home town five hundred miles away from this place.

As soon as the Leader saw me, he began to finish the Bible Study and he said, "Let's pray."

He began to pray for guidance from God. He then called me

down front. The other people in the room had not even heard us enter. I went down front and he had the Elders of the Fellowship come down also. And, he began to prophesy over me and to me, like I have never heard before or since. Now remember, I was raised in the Methodist Church. I did not know of such things.

I was thinking, "How can this be? This is confusion!"

I had no sooner thought that thought inside my head, when this man before me said, in the first person;

"THIS IS NOT CONFUSION, FOR I HAVE AUTHORED THIS, SAYETH THE LORD, AND IT SHALL SURELY COME TO PASS."

≈

That definitely got my full attention!

"I am issuing to you some things, says the Lord, that come only from My Kingdom, only from My Throne to you. Issuing unto you mandates, declarations.

It will be something to cause your heart even to perish within you.

Nevertheless, you shall live. Trust Me. Look to Me, for I have authored this, and it is not confusion.

I have predetermined to bring you into this place.

From this moment on, you will be put in areas where you will say, **'Thus saith the Lord'**.

My Word shall begin to burn within your heart, within your bosom.

Fire shut up in your bones. For I Am the Lord, and I have spoken. It shall surely come to pass."

The Lord told me, "You have a special love in your life.

I want you to give it up."

I knew right away what He was talking about.

"It was my art!" God knew that painting was my everything.

How could He ask such a thing of me?

He wanted to be my everything!

Then He said, "Because I want to use it. I would have you know that as you paint on canvas, and with your words that you are going to be painting on peoples' hearts, vivid pictures that they can see and understand and because of that, they will accept Me."

He said "Speak without reservation, without fear and wavering. Release the Word of the Lord and speak out. Do not compromise."

His Holy Spirit told me that my name will be cast out of many areas, but that my name is written in the Lamb's Book of Life.

"I will put you in some hard circumstances, but yet they are going to be very easy. People will say, 'That's too hard, it can not be, but My Spirit will be there to sustain."

This man of God prophesied over me for forty-five minutes. He laid my life before me, past, present and future.

He spoke as if he knew that I was an artist, but he could not have known this. He said "What you have been trying to do for the Lord is like someone trying to paint without stirring up the pigment in the bottom of the can of paint.

The Lord is going to be stirring and shaking up some things in your life so that what you are doing for Him will have deeper more colorful significance and meaning."

The prophet told me; "People will be going out of their way to miss the fellowship of you, but by this you will know that there is a great *calling* upon your life."

Little did I know that my life was really going to be shaken to its very core and nothing would ever be the same again.

The prophet said, "You will show God's people something of vision.

You will paint word pictures and by this people will know of the reality of God's Truth."

This man said that I was yet to do some of my greatest work in Jerusalem. He said that

I was to be anointed in the office of a prophet.

આ

He later told me that when I entered the room, that he had a vision of the Star of David over my head. I was amazed.

ॐ

You may recall that I bought an Israeli Flag in Jerusalem.

Well, as soon as I got back into my art studio after that trip, I took that Israeli Flag out of my suit case and hung it from the ceiling over my drawing board to get the wrinkles out of it.

So actually I was doing this series of paintings from Israel with the Star of David, (the sign of our Messiah) literally over my head.

At the end of that very special meeting, the Elders laid hands on me the receive the Baptism of God's Holy Spirit. At that time I didn't really understand fully what that entailed, but at that point in my life, I was ready to surrender all that I was to Him. I was also ready to receive everything that He had for me. Later, I started seeing a difference in my life because of God's Spirit.

On my way back across Texas, heading for home, God spoke to me.

"You have painted the Jerusalem of Jesus' time, and the Jerusalem of today. I want you to paint the Jerusalem that is yet to come, to edify and build up the people of God."

I waited for several weeks after that. I figured since I had never painted anything that I had not seen, that God was going to show me a vision.

Then God spoke to me saying,

"Jan, What are you waiting for?"

I replied, "Lord, I am waiting for you to show me, so I can do it."

He said **"I am waiting for you to do it, so I can show you."**

So often, I have learned that our ways are opposite of God's ways.

I painted the New Jerusalem on a canvas four feet wide and six feet high.

"New Jerusalem" by Jan Douglas Bish

I thought I was finished, but did not feel a release from the work. Then the idea came to me, to go back into the painting and put a rainbow around the Throne of God at the pinnacle of the city. Then I knew the painting was finished.

The painting was in progress for eight months. It was time for the unveiling of this Original. The place for the unveiling would be; The World Full Gospel Convention in New Orleans.

When the painting of the "New Jerusalem was revealed, a woman gasped and said:

"You painted my vision. Eight months ago God gave me a vision of the New Jerusalem, in New Zealand. You even painted the rainbow, just as I saw it."

You see, it was me who wanted the vision eight months ago, but none came to me. God gave the vision to a woman on the other side of the world and then brought us together for a confirmation to both of us, at the same time, at the unveiling of the original painting.

The series of works that I had named; "A Tour of Israel" became "A Tour of Israel and Beyond".

The number of paintings in this collection was seventeen. Each piece was finished and hung in the Bish Art Gallery with a sign that read "N.F.S." (Not for sale). Now, that really did not make sense because an art gallery has to have sales to survive. Here again, God wanted the series kept together.

When the last painting was done, God brought a man in off the street, once more, and into my gallery. He said; "I see the N.F.S, but I have been looking for a series of paintings just like this for a new hospital that I am building.

At that point in my life I was singing; "**You Light up my Life**" in a spiritual context.

There was to be a special Multi-Media Showing and Presentation of "A Tour of Israel and Beyond" at the Mariah Hotel in Te Aviv, Israel.

≈

A VISION OF ISRAEL:

While in Israel, the Lord showed me the love, compassion and sorrow that He felt for Israel and her people.

He placed this revelation deep within the depths of my spirit and soul.

It was in the middle of the night, at the Mariah Hotel, that I awoke with a start, and sensed a spiritual presence in the room.

I literally wept in the Spirit for more than two hours. It was deeper than anything that I had ever felt in my life.

My insides ached.

God spoke saying; "**My Words must be fulfilled. I have spoken and it must come to pass.**

In a vision, I saw the most beautiful girl I had ever seen. God told me that She was Jerusalem, created by His hands. Nobody could help but fall in love with her!

The Lord said to me, "You are My bride, the church, the Body of Christ, but don't ever forget that she was my first love, my intended. Don't ever say anything against her."

Then He showed me an old woman in her 80s and said, "Even though her face has changed many times through the years, and even though she has turned her back on Me and prostituted herself, her name is Israel and I still love her."

"On that day, you will realize that I am in My Father and you are in Me and, I AM IN YOU." *John 14:20*

For the first time in my life, I realized what that meant because He was in me and allowing me to feel as He felt.

That feeling of love and sorrow was deeper than anything I had ever felt.

෨

"When He, the Spirit of Truth comes, He will guide you into all TRUTH. He will tell you what is yet to come. He will bring glory to Me, taking from what is Mine and making it known to you." *John 16:12-15*

It was about six months later that the Lord God led me to a Scripture that I had not been familiar with previously. This Scripture more fully explained what God had told me in Israel, and it was also confirmation that I had heard Him correctly.

In the following verses of Ezekiel 16, God is describing Jerusalem as a beautiful young girl that has turned into a woman:

"I looked at you and saw you were old enough for love. I spread the corner of My garment over you and covered your nakedness.

I gave you My solemn oath and entered into a covenant with

you, declares the Sovereign Lord, and you became Mine.

So you were adorned with gold and silver, your clothes were of fine linen and costly fabric and embroidered cloth."

"Your food was fine flour, honey and olive oil.

YOU BECAME VERY BEAUTIFUL AND ROSE TO BE A QUEEN. And your fame spread among the nations on account of your beauty, because the splendor I had given you, made your beauty perfect, declares the Sovereign Lord.

BUT YOU TRUSTED IN YOUR BEAUTY AND USED YOUR FAME TO BECOME A PROSTITUTE. IN ALL YOUR DETESTABLE PRACTICES AND YOUR PROSTITUTION, YOU DID NOT REMEMBER THE DAYS OF YOUR YOUTH, WHEN YOU WERE NAKED AND BARE, KICKING ABOUT IN YOUR BLOOD.

WOE! WOE TO YOU, DECLARES THE SOVEREIGN LORD.

YOU HAVE DEGRADED YOUR BEAUTY.

THEREFORE I AM GOING TO GATHER ALL YOUR LOVERS, WITH WHOM YOU FOUND PLEASURE, THOSE YOU LOVED AS WELL AS THOSE YOU HATED. I WILL GATHER THEM AGAINST YOU FROM ALL AROUND AND WILL STRIP YOU IN FRONT OF THEM, AND THEY WILL SEE ALL YOUR NAKEDNESS.

I WILL PUT A STOP TO YOUR PROSTITUTION AND YOU WILL NO LONGER PAY YOUR LOVERS. THEN MY WRATH AGAINST YOU WILL SUBSIDE AND MY

JEALOUS ANGER WILL TURN AWAY FROM YOU; I
WILL BE CALM AND NO LONGER ANGRY."

JAN BISH KISSING THE ROCK WALL ABOUT THIRTY
FEET FROM THE HOLY of HOLIES, Jerusalem, Israel.

The Lord also spoke to me while I was in Israel, saying; "I
have placed you center stage to see My eternal drama
unfolding before your very eyes. But, with that privilege
comes responsibility."

I was on the hill of Megiddo over looking the Jezreel Valley
(the place of Armageddon), when suddenly the ground
began to shake beneath my feet. I heard thunder in my ears.
And I wondered, "IS THIS IT?" And, all of the sudden I
realized that what I was experiencing was two Israeli
Phantom Jets streaming down through the Valley breaking
the sound barrier.

While doing an art show in Cleveland, Ohio an elderly

gentleman approached me. "Are you Jewish?"

I told the man, "No."

He mentioned that he had noticed that I had so many paintings in my exhibit that I had done in Israel. So he asked me; "You do speak Yiddish don't you?"

I had to tell him that I didn't. He responded, "That's really strange because the name over your exhibit says; "Bish Art" You don't spell it quit like you do, but you would pronounce it exactly the same, Bishart means "One who is called out, an anointed one of God." And, I was thinking, "God is so awesome."

I had called my art work: Bish Art just because my name was Bish and it was my art. I felt like Abram when God had changed his name to Abraham (meaning father of many nations) so that every time he said his name he would be confessing that he was indeed the father of many nations. Like wise, for years, without knowing what I was truly saying, I was confessing that I was anointed by God and *called* to do what I was doing for Him. Every time I answered the phone; "Bishart". Every time I talked about my art work, I made that confession with my mouth.

If you confess with your mouth and believe in your heart, what ever you say shall come to pass.

During this period in my life God truly did take me "away from that which I knew best "I authored three books; "A New Revelation of Israel," "Trump your Trouble" and "So This is the Garden of Eden".

Television Talk Shows invited me to share what God was

doing in my life. There was "Zola Levett Live" out of Dallas, "Jewish Voice Broadcast" out of Arizona, "One Hundred Huntley Street" with David Mainse, across Canada and others.

JAN DOUGLAS BISH, TV TALK SHOW IN
SANTA BARBARA, CALIF.

Then there was one day that I felt led to study the Scriptures on evil spirits. I learned how to cast them out, where they go when they are cast out and when not to cast them out. And, what you do after you cast them out.

In other words, a rather complete study. I never knew much about this subject. The traditional churches, I had attended in my youth never taught on such things. Most people did not even believe in such things as evil spirits, just a figment of some peoples' imaginations. To be honest with you, I would much rather have remained innocent about such things.

But, the Lord had other plans for me.

The following week I was scheduled to speak at a

Presbyterian Church in a neighboring town. While I was speaking I noticed a young lady that slipped into the church auditorium. She arrived about fifteen minutes late and took a seat in the very last pew.

After I was finished speaking, I invited anyone who wanted, to come down for prayer. This young lady was the first one down the aisle. I asked her what her prayer request was and I only heard her mumble something. So it was unclear what she wanted.

I began to pray with God's Spirit. As I prayed, my hand was on her back. My eyes were closed. I at first felt her back tense, then turn cold, and even as though it was not flesh. I opened my eyes and saw her hands in front of her. The girl's hands looked arthritic and knolled. I didn't remember that, when she came down front. Then, I looked at her face and into her eyes. I noticed that I was looking directly at the incarnation of an evil spirit, face to face.

I had never seen anything like this in all my days. I didn't know if I was "in the spirit" and was just seeing something spiritually or if this manifestation had crossed over into the natural realm.

Then, another woman that was in our prayer circle spoke up. She said "What is your name?" And, I knew that this was a physical manifestation of an evil spirit because she was able to see it also.

I couldn't believe that the woman wanted to talk with this evil spirit.

I was wondering what was going to happen next? I was also beginning to think that I better take control of this situation.

Just then, this spirit spoke, saying in a low guttural voice through this girl's throat (just as it was in the Exorcist Movie) "I am HATE".

Right away I figured that my God is the God of Love.

This is the demon "Hate" This was not just a low ranking demon, but has to be Satan's right hand man.

My mind was running a mile a minute. I was thinking:

Just my luck. Oh sure this had to be the first time to face a demonic spirit, and his name has to be Hate. This is like taking a rookie off the bench, that has never played in the major leagues, on a real football field and facing him off against a team like the Steelers.

So, I said "In the Name of Jesus, I cast you out."

In that low guttural voice through clinched teeth the spirit said "NO".

Now, this part did not come up in my study. I knew and understood my authority. The Scriptures had taught me that all I had to do was cast out this foul spirit in "the Name of Jesus." All the spirits know that Name!

I was amazed! There is another Scripture that says, when you have done all to stand, stand therefore. So, I continued saying, "In the Name of JESUS, I cast you out."

Hate repeated, "NO."

And I said "What do you mean 'NO'? You have no choice, but to leave."

I could not believe that I was standing there arguing with an evil spirit. Well, after all I was dealing with Hate. Hate has to be one of the worst spirits to deal with.

Hate said "She needs me." I was just waiting for him to lie to me. I knew I had him now. I lorded it over him.

I looked this demon in the eye and said "You LIE! She does not need you and I COMMAND that you come out of her IN THE NAME OF JESUS!" This evil spirit knew that I was not playing around and that I understood my authority and was exercising my authority now. I was forceful and direct.

My hand was still on this young lady's back and I began to feel her relax, and then I felt her slump as the spirit left her. I then talked with this lady. She was twenty years old. I found out some more information. She had a very bad home environment. With a spirit as bad as the one she had harbored, I figured that she had to really be involved with witchcraft or the like. But **no**! She told me that she grew up in the Catholic Church.

Her brother had died during this past year and she was blaming God for his demise.

Then she told me "He (the evil spirit) did not want me to come today." Boy, that was an understatement!

This spirit was the reason why she was late and sat in the very back, of the church. If she had to, she could make a fast exit.

After I found out a few more things from this young lady, I covered her situation with prayer, so to speak; to sweep her house and clean up her situation so the spirit or spirits could not return. If the demonic spirits were allowed to return it would be seven times worse.

Also, if a person is not ready to let that spirit go, they will allow it to come back in, because they believe the lie, that they need that spirit. So be careful and do not just lightly go around casting out spirits. If you are unsure what to do, you can "bind "or render that spirit harmless, in Jesus Name, until you do know what to do. Then that person will not bring the spirits back on themselves.

About a year later I came across the woman that came late and sat in the back of the church. Her whole countenance had changed. She had a smile on her face. She truly had been delivered.

This experience taught me the reality of the dark spiritual side of this world that is all around us. They may be operating in a different dimension, but can strongly influence those of us in this realm. Those spirits desire to be part of this realm also. You would too if you were confined to that fifth dimension of separation from God.

These spirits desire to be embodied which is why they seek refuge where they may. When they are cast out they have to go to dry arid places (probably a description of the fifth dimension). They hate that.

Please take heart, and remember that there is more of us than there is of them. Only one third of the angelic force followed after Lucifer and became the demons that we have to contend with in this world today. We have two thirds of God's Warrior Angels on our side. And, we have the authority that is in the Name of Jesus. Understand who you are "In Him".

The Kingdom of God is at hand.

That means that it is all around you, so close you can reach out and touch it.

Another vision came; I saw myself standing alone. My spirit stepped out of my body and stood beside me. I noticed that my body was nothing more than an empty shell. The life was in my spirit, and my spirit looked just like me. My spirit stepped back in my body. Then I saw the Light of God and I saw that His Spirit looked just like Jesus. And then His Spirit stepped into my body. His Spirit was not some little substance that landed in the middle of my chest, but one that totally filled me from my finger tips to the top of my head, to the souls of my feet.

"All that I Am, is all that you are. When you sit, I sit. When you walk, I walk. What you say and what you hear goes directly into My Spirit. Do not grieve My Spirit."

Thus sayeth the Lord.

Joyce and I raised three beautiful daughters.

Our middle daughter, Dorinda died before her 29th birthday. Her name meant "little gift". One time when she was in high school she told me about one of her Jewish friends. Dorinda asked him why he was so happy and he said; "Today is "Yom Kippur," and my sins have been forgiven." She looked at him, smiled and said; "I begin every day that way."

You see Yom Kippur only comes once a year.

᭪

Our oldest daughter, Valarie, I often speak of her as my number one daughter. She has been a big help through the years in many different ways. She worked in our Christian Book Store and just about ran the Christian Art Publishing Company. Valarie also traveled across the country with me to do merchandising shows through the Christian Booksellers Association.

❧

Our third daughter, Valinda Janette was given all four of our names. **Valarie**, Do**rinda**, **Jan** and Joyce's middle name, An**nette**. She is a delight to know. And, I think she ended up with the best attributes from all four of us.

Joyce had married me right out of high school and never knew what it was like to be on her own. I tried to tell her that living alone was not what it is cracked up to be. I had been there, done that, and even bought the T-Shirt. She just had to try it!

Joyce told me after our kids were grown; "At least I am not leaving you for another man."

And I responded, "At least then there would be a reason. As it is, you are leaving me for no good reason at all."

I really did try to save my marriage. I realized of course that some of the fault had to be mine, but I didn't know how to put it back together. Joyce told me, "I just don't love you anymore." I wanted it to work, but by this time, I was angry, hurt, and I too had fallen out of love.

I think that "to love" is a choice that we make, but to God it is a command. Even as I have told my children, "Happiness is a daily decision."

"Lord, Your Word says that Love never fails." God said to me "**Love doesn't fail, people do.**" So I asked the Lord to fill me with His supernatural love for Joyce, and He did. But in some respects, I felt like that made my loss even greater, because I missed her even more. Now, God's love for her still flows, through me.

After my marriage seemed to just fall apart. I spent some dry years **looking for love** and trying to replace what I had lost. I missed raising kids and I missed having a mate. You might call those, my lost years.

I didn't have much to sing about, but I probably was singing the song; "Looking for Love in all the Wrong Places".

ॐ

It wasn't until I purposed in my heart to stop looking for love that I came across my next great love.

That was "a real trip" in my journey through this life.

I had gone to the theater by myself. After the movie, I decided to stop by and visit my number two daughter at work. (the one who would later be killed in a car accident.) At that time she was going to college learning how to develop new software programs for computers and working at Holiday Inn.

My daughter told me, when I saw her, that there was a "Parents without Partners" convention at the hotel and they were looking for someone to judge their art contest. My daughter told them that I was a professional artist, and she introduced me to the man in charge. I agreed to judge the art and they invited me to their dance at seven pm. the next evening.

BETTY JANE

The next night I showed up about seven-thirty. I saw the people who invited me and started for their table. On my way across the room I passed a young woman who was with another man.

We both did a "double take," but I kept on walking.

As the evening progressed, I had my eye on the lady, and I was wondering why the strange feeling of some sort of recognition. I also noticed that the guy she was with did not ask her to dance.

So, I went up to the guy and said; "Are you going to dance with this beautiful lady, or am I going to take her away from you? (that even surprised me, that it came out of my mouth)

Betty Jane looked up at me and said "Are you asking ME to dance?" Like, you better ask me, not the guy I'm sitting with.

So I addressed the question to her; "Would you like to dance?"

She said "Yes".

After that dance I went back to the table with my other new friends, but I kept an eye on Betty.

I asked the band if I could borrow one of their guitars and "sit in," on a number.

They said "Yes." And asked me "What key?"

I said "The key of C."

I would have dedicated this song to Betty, but there were several gals there with the same name.

That night "Blue Moon." was my song.

It was fast approaching midnight and I went over and asked Betty to dance once more.

While we were dancing to a slow romantic song, to the tune of "Good night my Love" I leaned down and kissed her lightly on her neck and said; "How 'bout we loose the guy your with, find the back door to this place and go get some breakfast?"

She said "What do you mean by that?" And, I said "There is a Kettle Restaurant across the street that starts serving breakfast at midnight."

She said "Oh, OK."

I think she thought that I was asking her for the whole night. That was not even on my mind, believe it or not. I have always been so naive.

My daughter told me later that the guy Betty was with, just looked around trying to figure out what had just happened. Actually, I was trying to figure out what was happening as well.

I took Betty Jane out for breakfast. Then I discovered that she was an artist with a degree in art from University of Texas and that she taught art at a local high school. I told her that I was a professional artist.

We agreed that we needed to see each other's work.

We figured that if we did not respect the other's work, then we could not respect each other.

You see, an artist is not only what you do, it's who you are. This was a Friday night (Saturday morning).

It took us two hours for breakfast and conversation and I made a date to meet her on the following Saturday.

A week from now.

I walked her out to her car. She was leaning against her car. I kissed her on the lips, once lightly, then again, a little more intense. NICE, maybe even some fireworks, down deep inside somewhere.

"ARE YOU THE ONE?"

(Betty confided in me a couple months later, that she had a really hard time getting to the dance that day. The water pump went out on her ranch and several other things happened to keep her away, but she knew that she had to be there at the Holiday Inn that night and nothing was going to stop her.)

She thought I would call her, that Saturday or even on Sunday. I was too busy trying to figure out what was happening. You know, I had made up my mind that I was not looking for love any more.

Then on Monday evening, I called her.

The first thing out of her mouth was,

"Are you the one?"

WOW, how does a guy answer that?

I think I just said "What do you mean by that?"

And she simply spoke the truth, no beating around the bush or playing little games that people play. She said "God told me that He was going to bring someone across my path. Are you that one?"

Looking back, I think I responded by saying

"I might be." or "Maybe I am."

From that time forward we were inseparable.

After our first date on that following Saturday night, we went to pick up her son, Patrick at the baby sitters. (His father had died when he was only about a year old.)

Patrick was now about two years old. He saw me, ran at me and jumped into my arms saying "DADDY!"

I looked at Betty and she said;

"Don't look at me, I didn't say **anything**."

BETTY and JAN   BETTY and PATRICK
HOLDING HANDS

Betty Jane's song was "Momma, He's Crazy" by the Judds. And we were in harmony, and of one mind.

Three months later I asked her to marry me. Actually I gave her a ring. She looked at it and said "What is this for?" Betty Jane then replied; "How could I refuse you, Patrick already had you picked out, and God told me you were coming."

Early on, we made up out minds that our relationship was the most important thing. If either one of us won an argument, we both would lose. You see, you cannot hurt the other person without hurting yourself, if you truly are one. She told me that she did not believe in divorce so I had better behave myself. The next eleven years together was like a honeymoon.

We were stopped by a teenage girl one time in the Shopping Mall. She said, "I just saw you two holding hands and I thought to myself, that's the kind of marriage I would like, the kind of relationship where you are still in love after all those years." She added "How long have you been married?"

I had to tell her "Only three months, but it will be the same after 50 years." We must have looked OLD to her.

Shortly after we came together, Betty Jane had a dream which she related to me. Neither one of us understood the dream. She dreamed that she and Patrick were on one side of a bridge. I came across the bridge to join them. And, then Patrick and I came back across that bridge *alone.*

Eleven years later we understood the dream when Betty was attacked by cancer and died at the age of forty-seven.

She also had some dark dreams about demonic forces coming out of a river to get her. We of course came against those dreams because we felt like it was a warning of danger. I have discovered that when you are involved in spiritual warfare, that there are casualties. Betty had put up a fierce fight with the evil one for more than a year. The evil one came to steal, kill and destroy.

Betty went home to be with the Lord to claim her victory. And I understood why I brought Patrick back across that bridge, without Betty.

She passed over to the other side in October of 2000. She is sorely missed by all who knew her. At the end, I told Betty Jane; "I can not stand your pain any more, and I know that you can't. It is time for you to go be with Jesus." I saw one tear fall from her eyes and within a half hour, she was gone. I wiped that tear away, kissed her and gently closed her eyes to this dimension of life.

There was a secular song that was very spiritual to me. Through the years it has meant a lot, when I needed to hear these words. This is my love story and this is my song unto the Lord who has brought me through my rough and lonely times, after annulment, after divorce and after death of a beloved mate.

"I cried a tear. You wiped it dry. I was confused. You cleared my mind. I sold my soul, You bought it back for me and held me up and gave me dignity. Somehow You needed me.

You gave me strength to stand alone again, to face the world out on my own again.

You put me high upon a pedestal, so high that I could almost see Eternity.

You needed me. You needed me.

And, I can't believe it's You. I can't believe it's true. I needed You and You were there.

And I'll never leave. Why should I leave? I'd be a fool, cause I've finally found someone who really cares.

You held my hand when it was cold. When I was lost, You took me home.

You gave me hope when I was at the end and turned my lies back into truth again, You even called me friend. You needed me." And, I need You.

PATRICK'S MOM HAD JUST TOLD HIM TO "STRAIGHTEN UP" FOR THIS PICTURE.
WE ARE IN THE DRESSING ROOM AT THE PASSION PLAY, READY TO GO ON STAGE.

&

Betty Jane was an accomplished artist, and actress in The Great Passion Play.

She was a docent at the Sacred Arts Center, and also worked as a guide in The New Holy Land Tours of Eureka Springs, Arkansas.

Patrick and his Dad at the Play.

We just about raised Patrick in The Great Passion Play. He started out as a "Lantern Boy" for Nicodemus, became a member of the Sanhedrin Guard and then the Head Guard before he left for University.

Betty Jane Bish is a member of The Great Passion Play Hall of Honor, and even more important, her name is written in "The Lamb's Book of Life."

Trying to learn how to live alone once more, I read several books that were recommended. I went through the motions and exercises of "treat yourself by going out to eat alone,"

"Go to an amusement park alone.," etc. But the pain was so great that I was thinking, I would never want to go through that ever again.

Original Painting "The Market Place" by Jan Douglas Bish

I did not want to leave any one else behind me to grieve like I did.

I could not bring myself to paint for what seems like a very long time. I had lost my inspiration to create.

IT'S NOW MANY YEARS LATER

And, I was trying to figure out why I still felt half dead inside.

The following is a question the Lord asked me. He said:

"What did you do in the physical world when Betty became ill?"

That got me to thinking. I closed up our home, took Patrick and went to be with Betty for treatment in Baltimore, Maryland. After that we had to go to Charlotte, North Carolina and then finally to a Cancer Research Center in San Antonio, Texas. All of this encompassed one year.

I home schooled Patrick on a laptop computer in airports, hospitals and in our travel trailer.

After Betty passed on, Patrick and I took a short respite before we headed home to Eureka Springs, Arkansas.

The house had been abandoned for a year and it took Patrick and I, a while to clean it up. I rented out the residence side to create some much needed income, and I made the commercial side of our building, where we had an art gallery, LIVABLE.

That is exactly what happened to me in the spiritual realm of my existence. The half of my life (house) where Betty and I lived was left vacant. I closed that half of my life. I boarded the windows and doors where no light could even come in and I lived in the shadows on the other side for a while.

The other half of my life, I have made very livable and comfortable.

I did not see any reason to reopen that old half of my life again. I was happy with who I was and what I was doing. After all, there was only myself to please and I was content. I did not need any more space.

I have met new friends and they have been trying to get me to open the other half of my life again. Right now, all I have done is take the boards off the doors and windows. I have not brought myself to the point where I want to reenter that other side of my house.

It will take time and energy to clean it up and make it presentable. And, God must direct my path.

I poured myself into working at The Great Passion Play in Eureka Springs, Arkansas.

Jan Bish as: Simon Peter, walking on the Sea of Galilee

Jan Bish as: Ciaphas the High Priest, in the Play

I have played five different roles in The New Holy Land which is part of the same ministry of The Great Passion Play in Eureka Springs, Arkansas.

The Play is five nights a week and the Holy Land consumed my days.

My friends and co-workers are like family to me.

And, like Crocodile Dundee said in his first movie; "Me and God, we be mates."

We have a personal relationship with the Lord of Lords.

I am reminded of the time in elementary school, when I was "playing a role, and the cameras were always rolling."

(I can see now where God uses all things to the good, for those who love Him.)

LIGHT AND SHADOW

TRUTH AND REALITY

I want to know the difference between Light and Shadow, Truth and Reality. I want to know where one ends and the other begins, or even if there actually is no ending and it all just flows together into infinity.

My mind and spirit desire to experience the different dimensions of God and understand the spirit realm and how it interacts with humanity in this physical world. My whole life has lead me to this moment in time.

An artist's life is full of light and shadow. If his paintings don't have enough light they are flat, boring and without the brilliance of color they should have. If there is not enough light, there are no shadows and where there is no shadow, there is no depth and everything seems flat and depressing.

So we need to live with Light and Shadow.

Look at Truth as God, and truth as the spirit realm. You should understand that the spirit realm is even more real than the reality that you have known.

The reality that you have known in the past is physical. Some people don't think things are real unless they can touch it, smell it, or see it.

Think about power for instance, electricity.

You can not see it, but the results of it are all around you.

Oh sure it can be examined and explained, but you already know that it is real.

What I would like to show you is that the spirit realm is just as real and even more powerful than the physical world that you can see. I would like to show you all of God's creation and how it interacts at different dimensions and can even cross over from one dimension to another.

I want you to see how it all ties together, how that Scarlet Thread of "String Theory" is woven through out the fabric of this universe. Understand, how it is all tied together and held in place.

All of my life's personal experience has lead me to see these truths and understand them. It is the Truth that has lead me here, not my realities.

As you have seen in my life. My realities were always changing. Is it good to know that there is a realm that never changes and that realm is the same, today, yesterday and forever.

LET US NOW BEGIN ANOTHER JOURNEY

Please keep an open mind and judge all things according to Scripture. The following is not what you were taught in Sunday School through the traditional church, as a child. But, now it is time to put away childish things and grow up into a mature believer. It's time to sit under some mature teaching.

Do not fight against a theory, just because it is new, and the concept is old. Accept the deeper things of God and His creation.

Did you not know that in the end times that knowledge will increase? Not just physical knowledge!

This is a journey into the past. We need to understand the past before we can go into the future. That is why I started this book with my birth. My being born and my life's experience is what brought me to this point.

Keep an open mind and allow your imagination the freedom to experience new thought, instead of the old theology.

When I was ready to commence with Biblical Truth (Truth and Reality).God told me once more to start with "In the Beginning". You need to understand the beginning before you will grasp the reasons why the world is like it is today. The things that you are now facing are a direct result of the past.

All the while I was anxious to get into the future Truths that God had shared with me about Who He is and where He lives and the way He constructed the universe as we know it, so we could live better, more aware and constructive lives.

This will be a journey from the Biblical Truth of

"In the Beginning" (Gen. 1), to the ultimate reality of quantum physics theory.

You will travel from the "earth that then was" to "the earth that now is".

This will be a quantum leap of faith into the spiritual reality of infinity and beyond.

"In the beginning God created the heaven and the earth."

The **spirit realm** and the **dry land**.

When was the "BEGINNING? Does it really matter?

Happenings are not measured by time in God's Realm.

He just knows when the "time" is right!

It was in God's heart and mind to create by the power of His Word. He spoke it and there it was; a new solar system. Heavens (Spirit realm) and Dry Land (which is what earth means.)

And He would create people as an extension of His love.

Now we are talking ages past.

God's angels were not *given* free will, but He would create His people with free will and they would give God much pleasure. He would create a beautiful place on the Dry Land for His new creation and would send His most beautiful Angel (Lucifer) into the Earthly Domain, to watch over His Garden.

So Lucifer was given an Earthly throne with authority in the earth, subject to God's authority of course.

Col. 1:16, It is clear that there are thrones, principalities and powers in Heaven and in the earth, visible and invisible. It should not be difficult then to believe that Lucifer was given one of these thrones and a kingdom to rule over before "his fall from Grace ".

You will recall when Lucifer took Jesus "up into a high mountain, showed Him all the kingdoms of the world in a moment of time. And the devil, Lucifer said unto Him, all this power will I give thee, and the glory of them: for that is delivered unto me: and to whomsoever I will, I will give it." *Luke 4:6*

Lucifer no doubt had in his mind how wonderful it would be to rule over all the earth. Why he would be just like God, himself. You see; Lucifer's kingdom was on the earth in a pre-Adamite period indicated by the fact that he ascended up to heaven (that higher spiritual realm or dimension) for the revolt (with one-third of all the angels and Satan had the loyalty of the people on the earth over which he ruled.) And, the devil Lucifer, Satan was returned to the earth after his fall. You see he was already in the Garden before Adam and Eve.

God later was to tell Lucifer that he had (spoken in his heart) This is a way of communication in the spirit realm.

"I will ascend to Heaven; I will raise my throne above the stars of God. I will sit enthroned on the mount of assembly, on the utmost heights of the sacred mountain. I will ascent above the tops of the clouds; I will make myself like the Most High." *Isaiah. 14:14*

The fall of Satan and the fall of the pre-Adamic Race is seen as the direct result of the judgment of *Gen. 1:2 that* came to the earth,

"And the earth became a wasteland and empty."

Jeremiah 4:23-29 "I beheld the earth and indeed it was without form and void. And the Heavens they had no light. I beheld the mountains and indeed they trembled and all the hills they had moved back and forth.

I beheld and the fruitful land was a wilderness, and all it's cities were broken down at the presence of the Lord and by His fierce anger.

For thus says the Lord; The whole land shall be desolate; yet I will not make a full end. For this shall the earth mourn and the heavens above be black. Because I have spoken."

This is not speaking about the flood of Noah's time. This language puts us back to *Gen. 1-2*. "The earth was (became) without form and void; darkness was on the face of the deep."

Lucifer was set up with a throne on earth, and his pride lead him to slander God and lead all the people, the Pre-Adamic

Race, away from God and even convinced one-third of the angels to revolt with him. (this is the demonic force at work in the world, even today). Just one more dimension of the spiritual realm.

All life was destroyed in the world of Pre-Adam. The word "was" in Genesis, verse 2 is the verb "to be" confirms that the earth "became" waste and empty.

The phrase "without form" in verse 2 translates in other Scriptures as "vain, confusion, empty, nothing."

God did not create the earth in such a waste and ruined condition, which was stated in *Isaiah 45:18.* "He is a Rock, His work is perfect; for all His ways are justice."

Deut. 32:4 and Eccl. 3:11 "He has made everything beautiful."

The earth was created "Dry Land" not flooded. The flood was a curse, not a creative act.

Darkness and floods were revealed to be the result of judgment. All predictions of future darkness also depicts judgment.

There are many differences in Scriptures concerning the Pre-Adam Flood and Noah's Flood. Definitely two different catastrophic floods are recorded in Scripture.

Gen. 1:1 Original creation made perfect and inhabited (*Isaiah. 45:18*) "The world that then was" 2*nd*. *Peter 3:5-8* and "the world that now is," two different systems.

It was at this time in *Gen. 1:2-3* that God recreated "this world that now is" in 6 days. Beginning with the words "And the Spirit of God moved upon the face of the waters. And God said let there be light." He rested on the 7th day.

God created and placed Adam and Eve in the Garden. Because He did create the earth to be inhabited.

God told them to "Be fruitful and multiply, and REPLENISH the earth, SUBDUE IT; and have DOMINION OVER EVERY LIVING THING UPON THE EARTH." *Gen. 1:28*

Gen. 1 :28 tells Adam to "<u>replenish</u>" the earth, not to just plenish it. That means that there was people here before. So, moving with envy and jealousy over God's new creation with authority and dominion, Lucifer was already in the Garden on the earth.

So Lucifer brought about the downfall of this new earth ruler, Adam, at least that was his plan.

Why all this desire to usurp man's dominion of the earth? Earth **WAS** Lucifer's Domain. This is also why he went after every man of God from that time forth.

Always remember that YOU, as a believer have full authority over Lucifer and his demonic force, and nothing will by any means hurt you.

You have been given authority over serpents, scorpions and over all the power of the enemy,

IN THE NAME OF JESUS!

That authority can not be taken from mankind again.

In the beginning God created the heaven and the earth. No one really knows when the BEGINNING was. Personally I don't care if it is 10 billion years old or ten thousand. As I have said before, "Time stands still at the speed of Light and Our God is Light."

When Scientist really do discover the age of this earth. It will completely agree with the Scriptures. In other words, there is no reason why, if science is proven and Scripture is true, that they should not agree.

Even now, progressive thinking physicists and Scripture are so very close.

Lucifer had already ruled the earth and became a fallen angel before Adam and his race.

Adam and Eve were not the first ones on this planet. Satan fell with the Pre-Adamic Race in judgment because of his rebellion. Lucifer actually invaded Heaven *from* the earth. (*Isaiah. 14:12-14*)

Ezek. 28:11-17 gives us a picture of Lucifer before he fell from Grace. "Protector of the earth, full of wisdom, perfect in beauty," as ruling in the Garden of Eden (before Adam).

All of this I say, so that you will better grasp the significance of the lost authority, regained by Jesus for us.

We should be learning how to rule and reign with Jesus, NOW.

God wants you to understand spiritual truth, NOW.

We all know the rest of the story God showed His new

creation (the first Adam) through the beautiful garden He had prepared for them. Gave them instructions, supplied them with food, water, gold, etc.

That is also God's will for you today. He is the same, yesterday, today and forever.

You will remember in the Garden of Eden that Lucifer questioned the woman about what God had said.

Eve answered saying; "God hath said" which is the way we should also respond to Satan's whispers in our ears. Eve continued with what God had told her about eating the fruit of the tree in the midst of the garden:

"Neither shall you touch it, lest you die." Lucifer came back with the same old line he still uses, trying to cast doubt on God's word. "Surely not!"

They blew it! Don't you!!

So what does all of this have to do with you? You need to understand that Satan had control of this earthly realm, when God originally assigned Lucifer to be a caretaker of His Garden in the ageless past.

Lucifer tried to raise his throne above the throne of God and revolted with one-third of the angels and the Pre-Adam Race. That caused God's judgment of Flood and Darkness over the earth that was originally created to be inhabited from the very beginning. The cities fell, ALL men died, Lucifer was cast down with the third of the angels that followed him.

Later, after Judgment and Lucifer's fall, "the Spirit of God moved upon the face of the waters" and God said "Let there be light," when God placed Adam and Eve in the Garden of Eden, they were given authority over all the earth. That upset Lucifer because he figured that it still belonged to him.

So, Lucifer regained the authority from Adam, causing Adam's fall from grace.

Jesus came to regain that lost authority back for us. Satan tried to tempt Jesus, by offering Jesus all the kingdoms of this world saying that they were his to give.

Jesus of course knew the Truth, because He is the Truth.

Satan killed Jesus without a legal right to do so.

Jesus willingly laid down His life for us.

For three days before the resurrection, Jesus "Lorded it over them" in Hell. (That lowest spiritual realm or dimension that is separated from God.) Now our authority is through Jesus.

He told us "Therefore YOU go," part of our great commission, with His Power of Attorney.

And, continue to Lord that Authority over Satan and his demonic brood till the end of time. (Time as we know it.)

GENISIS to REVELATION

Revelation 12: 1 - 5 **First coming of Jesus (the last Adam) to this Physical Realm from the Spiritual Realm.**

"REVELATION TWELVE" BY JAN DOUGLAS BISH

"And there appeared a great wonder in Heaven; a woman clothed with the sun. (This is Israel) The moon under her feet and upon her head a crown of twelve stars. (twelve tribes of Israel)

And, being with child, cried, travailing in birth. (the birth of Jesus) and pained to be delivered.

And there appeared another wonder in Heaven, and behold a great red dragon (Lucifer), having seven heads and ten horns and seven crowns upon his heads, and his tail drew the third part of the stars of Heaven (one-third of the angelic force that fell with Satan in his fall - that became the demonic forces that roam the earth.) and did cast them to the earth: and the dragon stood before the woman (Israel) which was ready to be delivered for to devour her child (Jesus) as soon as it was born.

And she brought forth a male child that was to rule all nations with a rod of iron: and her child was caught up unto God (the crucifixion, Resurrection and Ascension) and to His throne."

The coming together of science

ADVANCED PHYSICS THEORY, AND THE SPIRITUAL REALM

When you understand the String Theory, you will be able to unravel the mysteries of time, dimensions, space and infinity, the place where God abides. And then, you will even begin to comprehend your own little universe better.

The crux of String Theory:

We are not going to get involved in the technical aspects of String Theory. I just want you to understand the concepts.

It was thought initially that there were many different string theories but now the physicist are beginning to agree that they have all been looking at the same thing from different perspectives. What some thought to be discrepancies were nothing more than opposing forces.

One force will balance out the other force. Keeping nature in balance is a delicate matter, but God knows all about that. God has orchestrated the universe with vibrating strands of energy that holds all things together.

These strings of energy are like rubber bands that stretch and vibrate, up and down and side ways.

When you look at a diamond from different perspectives the

facets reflect and refract the light differently, but it is still but one diamond.

There are twenty different elements in this universe. The power and force of each one is a delicate mathematical balancing act. If only one element is slightly off, the universe and it's equation (equilibrium) collapses.

There are up to eleven different dimensions, a universe where everything is made up of "string". String is what holds the atoms and particles together. There are parallel worlds operating within and beside each other at different dimensions.

We are only separated from the Spiritual Realm because they travel at the speed of Light within different dimensions and we operate under the law of TIME and gravity. This also explains why you can not see the spirit realm when you are living in the twenty-four hour day, within the dimension of time, and held down by gravity.

This is not the Science Fiction of the 50s.

It's String Theory and it is for this Century.

String Theory may well be very theoretical. It is an effort to tie together the four forces of the universe. Included is **Gravity, Electro/Magnetic,** as well as the **weak** and **strong** nuclear forces. Ten or eleven (depending on who you talk to) dimensions are mathematically concluded. The forces in space and time (as we know it) are horizontal, vertical, forward and back.

In the past we have only known of three dimensions, or four. The fourth dimension being, time.

We are traveling through a segment of that fourth dimension now, and living in a three dimensional world.

When God called on me to share these things with you, it was my first response to say (as we all do),

"WHY ME?" Why don't You go talk to a Physicist, they will comprehend what you are talking about, I know nothing of such things.

As if I could tell God what He needed to do!

He simply answered, saying,

"Because I want to talk to you."

String Theory attempts to provide a complete, unified, and consistent description of the fundamental structure of our universe. It has been referred to as the "Mother of all theories".

So, if string theory is correct, the entire world is made of strings!

Perhaps the most remarkable thing about string theory is that such a simple idea works for the scientists, and does not clash with Christian beliefs.

God would say to you:

"I Am the Truth, The Way and the Light. I Am the String Theory that holds all things together. I have used the small insignificant, simple things of this world to confound the wise."

You can not get much smaller than "String Theory".

I love it! The smallest thing in this universe turns out to be the biggest discovery of this century. It is the very smallest things in this universe that prove intelligent design over Darwinism's theory of "Chance". When you understand how an individual human cell operates and multiplies from the inside out you have to believe that it's one of God's best ideas and creations. Definitely "design," not "chance".

We thought we were so smart when we discovered the Atom, then the Particles and now the latest thing that scientists are working on, "String Theory". Truly a journey through Light and Shadow to the infinite Truth, and the secrets of the universe.

There are **TWO REALMS**:

Heaven and Earth (in traditional terms)

Within those Realms there are different dimensions. The two Realms are side by side at different levels or different dimensions. From the physical realm you can not see the spiritual because (once more) they are traveling at the speed of Light and we are traveling in time.

The spirit realm is not contained or restrained with time and gravity, and we are.

This explains the interaction of the Spirit Realm and the Physical Realm. In the spiritual world you may be able to just think of being there, and there you are. (mental telepathy)

This is also how we communicate with the spiritual realm

from the physical realm (prayer).This is one of the ways we hear from God and this is the method that Lucifer uses to whisper in our ears.

We are all here together. This is a world of dualism.

Parallel worlds (Realms in different dimensions).

Understanding that the Spirit Realm and Physical Realm are realities that operate in the same space in a different dimension of space and time. (A parallel world.) Principalities and powers in the spirit realm and in the earth, visible and invisible.

You are living your natural life in the shadow of the Light from the Spiritual Realm.

Then again, you are more spiritual than you are physical. Your spirit has not changed since you have stepped into your physical body. Your body and your soulish realms have changed and grown.

All you have to do is look into a mirror and you will see that the physical side of you has changed. As for me, I don't really like looking into a mirror to see the changing reality around me. I prefer to think about my changeless spirit that feels the same as I did when I was eighteen. Sometimes I feel like I go around in circles, but that's okay.

God likes circles. He created the domains in which we live, and in His Word, refers to it as the **circle** of the earth. God likes wheels and circles. To know that, all you have to do is look around this beautiful universe, it's full of them. So, if the physicists are correct with these new theories, then the circle of the earth continues at different levels and dimensions within the circles. God's creation is all woven together with the fabric of string to infinity.

No matter where you are on this earth, there is nothing blocking your path from continuing your journey.

Yes, you will have to cross mountains, sail the oceans and climb walls, but man has always been able to do that.

Only our own imaginations can stop us from being the kind of voyager that God wants us to be.

Our own reality; We are the center of our own universe and all the other planets (people) rotate around us, in our own thinking. The smaller we are, the bigger the universe, therefore when you consider the smallest part of a **"particle"** you have entered the space of "infinity".

When you travel at the speed of light, you have entered infinity and you are with God.

So all of this takes us back to TRUTH and REALITY.

Have you noticed yet? This all goes in circles and cycles. "What goes around comes around". "Love makes the world go 'round." etc.

We actually do live our "circle of life" in both realms at the same time, side by side.

What if you were traveling through time (which you are) and you pass through the spiritual realm that is traveling at the speed of light in the opposite direct? Your physical eyes might miss it or just see it as a blur of **Light and Shadow**, if you see anything at all.

Some people do have spiritual experiences and do see portions of that spirit realm. Some see it in visions, some in dreams. You might find these things in the sixth dimension.

Paul, when writing to the Corinthians mentioned that he was taken to the third heaven (that third spiritual dimension or that seventh dimension, counting from this realm).

We live in three dimensions and the fourth is time.

The fifth dimension is spiritual warfare, the sixth could be dreams and visions.

Paul was taken to the seventh dimension out of eleven dimensions (the third Heaven).

Paul said he didn't know if he was "in the body or out of the body". Spiritual experiences are like that. I too, do not talk about such things to glory in myself, but to lift up the Truth to you. Actually it must have been an "out of the body" experience because he would have had to leave gravity and time behind him in order to enter the spiritual realms.

Do you think Paul is strange because he had an "out of the body experience"? Remember to test all truth by Scripture and don't judge others "strange" because they have also had similar experiences.

Have you ever just partially awakened from a dream?

You were still in that place of dreams and visions, but you could hear the sounds and smell the smells of earth? Wake up and smell the coffee! At that moment, did you feel like you had one foot in the spiritual realm and the other foot on dry land? Perhaps, one of the spiritual dimensions around us is the place of dreams and visions.

Have you ever had the thought, which was real?

Was the dream your reality or being awake?

Which did you want to be true?

I am speaking of your good dreams, of course. Your bad dreams come from that dimension of spiritual warfare, that lowest spiritual dimension, where Satan and the demons abide.

One of my conversations with God....

Jan: "Why are you talking to me about quantum physics - I know nothing of such things."

God: "Because that is where I live"

Jan: "Shouldn't you be talking to a physicist?"

God: "I want to talk to you... I want you to remain fluid. I will take you to new heights. I will show you mysteries and you will understand."

I was having a little trouble understanding what God meant when He told me to remain "FLUID".

I had talked this over with friends. You can always tell when they don't understand what you are saying because their eyes kind of glaze over and they get this "far a way" look.

Probably wishing that they were "far away" from you. That's okay, because I know that I have always been "way out there". I have grown accustomed to "living on the edge" and God loves me the way I am.

Anyway, I felt like the Lord finally said to me. "If you don't understand a word, just look it up."

Now, doesn't that just sound like a Teacher? I know because I was married to one!

So, I did look up that word. I was amazed to find out that FLUID is a term in physics.

Isn't that interesting, since you will recall that God had already told me, that was where he lived.

Well, I found it interesting! This is what the word; <u>FLUID</u> meant....<u>physics</u> : a substance such as a *liquid* or gas whose molecules <u>flow freely</u>, so that it has <u>little resistance to pressure.</u>

I looked up RESISTANCE and found out that was another word used in physics. It meant a force that opposes or slows down another force; opposition to the flow.

I needed to clear my mind and focus on the simple truth of what God was showing me. All this meant was, that I was to **flow freely** in the things that God had shown me, with little resistance to pressure. I needed to **stop resisting** what **God** was telling me, open my mind to new thought. It meant that I should not be a force that opposed and slowed down the force of God in this realm, but that I was to flow with Him.

Now you know how my thinking process works. I need to

analyze things until I understand.

The Spiritual Force that I am talking about is kind of like when **one** person prays, they have the ability to send out one thousand angels. If you have TWO IN AGREEMENT you can send out TEN THOUSAND angels on assignment. Just look at the difference between the power of one and the power of two, in agreement within the spiritual realm. Do the math! Make your own equation!

Scientists are used to this way of thinking, but I am not a scientist.

It is more difficult for me.

It's easier to accept the things that we were taught in Sunday School by people who were spiritually ignorant.

Sorry about that!

Even though they were well meaning, they did not get with God, delve into His Word and dig out the truth for themselves, or for you.

It's called spiritual exercise! It is my hope that I will be able to enlighten your understanding and stir your interest so that you will know that you too are more spiritual than you think you are.

Once you realize that you are more spiritual than you are physical, then you will have a better, more REAL relationship with God. You will know how the spirit realm influences the physical realm. And, if we grasp that concept we will know how to live a better more productive life.

Once you know these things, then you too may live "where God lives." Wouldn't you like to live where God lives? He lives in the midst of a prism of bright colorful light, a place where white light turns into a spectrum of colors like you have never seen before. He lives at the speed of light because HE IS THE LIGHT. More colorful than anything you could even imagine. But, God wants you to use your imagination anyway. That's what it's there for.

God's ways are higher (or deeper) than our ways. We really should not lean unto our own understanding, but take all things to God and learn how to listen. "Harkin unto the voice of the Lord". Delve into His Word.

Before I go any further, I know that I have used the term "REALM" a lot.

This is actually what that word means:

The scope of something. A particular or stated area,

A domain. An area of interest or study.

A Realm is a

KINGDOM RULED BY A MONARCH.

(1)   The Spirit Realm of God rules over the spiritual and the physical realms from the Highest Spiritual Dimension. Jesus is the King of Kings.

(2)   Satan has his government organized and set up in Principalities within the dimension where he now exists. Since he was cast down, with one-third of the angels. This is a lowest spiritual dimension, separated from God.

(3)   And, the governments of man rule in this physical realm with authority granted from God. Now, if you understand your spiritual authority and the right to legally use the Name of Jesus, then you may also rule over Satan's Domain that is located in the lowest spiritual dimension.

So every time I have spoken of the different REALMS, this is the order of their existence.

FORMS OF DUELALITY

The following is a comparison of Light and Shadow, truth and reality, spirit and physical, Heavens and Earth. This view is from the perspective of quantum physics.

Let's look at some things that we are already familiar with, from a deeper level or perspective.

<u>Light</u>
*no time
*no gravity
* changeless

<u>and Shadow</u>
*time and gravity
*always changing

<u>Truth</u>
*no time
*no gravity
* changeless

<u>and Reality</u>
* time and gravity
*always changing

<u>Spirit</u>
*no time
*no gravity
* changeless

<u>and Physical</u>
* time and gravity
*always changing

My song now is AMAZING GRACE as well as my mother's theme song during her life in this realm; "How Great Thou Art"

Let us reason together and recount what we have learned.

We know that there are two Realms.

(Heaven and Earth). We also are familiar with the dimensions within the physical realm. If you would care to assume that there are eleven dimensions in God's creation, the Seventh level or dimension of (the spirit realm) Heaven would be the place where God resides. That would make the lowest spiritual level, (just the other side of time) or the fifth dimension, the place of Satan's abode with his demonic spirits (a place of separation from God).

No one really knows what God uses all these other dimensions for, but I want you to imagine each dimension woven into the fabric of this universe and tied together with the String Theory. Imagine that all of these levels are co-mingled with the realm in which you now live.

These different dimensions could be light years away, or more than likely so close we could reach out and touch someone.

The Spirit realm could be right next door because there is no measurement of time as we know it in the spiritual dimensions.

There is nothing wrong with imaginations. God gave us our imaginations so that we could THINK beyond that which we could only see with our physical eyes. Just because you imagine something, that does not mean that it is not real. Let us open up our minds and expand the universe with it. Don't be content to live in your little corner. God wants you to grow into a spiritual being, more every day. Why? Because He wants you to know, where He lives.

God wants you to expand where you live, and live your life on a higher, deeper plane, a higher level of REALITY.

Be all that you can be. Join God's Army. Become so spiritual that when you pass over to that other spiritual dimension, it will be like passing through a sheer curtain.

Have you ever had the feeling that you have been there before? Have you ever revisited a place in the past (and it seemed so real to you.), a place where time does not exist for you? It is as though you are traveling down the physical road of your life through that fourth dimension of time.

The past is the road behind you and your future is in front of you. Have you ever seen into your future? Some people have, you know. I have been to all of these places in my life. God wants you to come for a visit some time.

Perhaps you will find all of these things in just another Spiritual Dimension, so close to the realm in which you now live. "So close and yet, so far."

These dimensions are all within the grasp of Quantum Physics which requires that "Leap of Faith".

Is there no end to the power of God and all that He can imagine for all of us, to live deeper lives?

What would life be without imagination, dreams, visions and fantasy? It would be HELL, because that is what it would be like to be separated from God. It would be like living in the same realm as Satan and his demon spirits, a hot, dry arid place.

The more spiritual things that you understand, the more you

understand the things around YOU. You begin to see why this has happened and why that happened. You will understand why bad things happen to good people, and how God can use ALL things for the good, to those who love Him.

The world will make better sense to you and you will be more comfortable. You know the saying,

"The best surprise is no surprise."

Life can be easier if you know what is around the next bend of the road.

There will always be mystery, as long as we live in this realm, but that is also a good thing, it keeps us interested. We all love a good mystery, don't we? I know that I do.

We have been on a very long journey over a very short period of time. What have we learned?

You should always learn from a good teacher or from your own experience. Sometimes we even have to learn from our own mistakes, but that's the hard way to learn. What ever we learn along the way has to be checked and be in accordance with God's Word. The Bible is the final authority. If, what you have learned, does not line up with the Word of God, you better rethink your situation and your position.

If you do not have a source of invariable Truth, you have to live in the Shadows and stumble around in the dark because you haven't got a clue. You need the Light of Truth to guide you along your path through this life.

Always remember that there are deceiving spirits at hand. They will lie to you and try to guide you down the wrong path.

You have been through my life and you know that I base all this information on Revelations from God (judged according to Scripture), my life's experience, and some good teachers along the way. I have learned from my bad experiences and prospered from the good.

The most important things that I have learned, came from the Word of God.

Now, I see the reason "Why me?" I did not have any wrong thinking to get in the way. I did not have any thinking at all in this realm of thought. I was a blank page on which He could write. I could learn how to be FLUID and flow with God instead of slowing Him down. He had told me many years before, that He would enable me to paint word pictures so His people would be edified and would see and understand the deeper things of God because of the things that He placed in my life.

My life has been shaken and stirred, and those experiences

have made me a stronger, more understanding person.

I hope that this journey has opened your eyes to see the Truth of God that is all around you. Truly as Jesus said, "The Kingdom of God IS at hand."

Beware of that lower spiritual dimension and realm of influence.

Do not be deceived or mislead down the wrong path of life. Understand your authority in the earth!

GOD'S MUSIC

Oh, by the way....

Did you know that God is INTO music?

I play several stringed instruments myself.

Self taught! I have always loved music.

I heard some kids talking the other day, and they were saying; "GOD ROCKS!" They probably didn't realize how true that statement was.

I know that He is my Rock, my stronghold. It's nice to know that He is not in some far off La La Land, but right here with us. Just across a thin veil that we can not see through, but His Place is more real than this physical realm.

Our God really must enjoy the sounds of a string quartet. The entire universe is God's stringed instrument, playing sweet music that emanates from the vibrating strings and strands of energy called "String Theory".

Talk about a "high energy" sound! God's creation has rhythm, delicate balance and is well tuned. His music is beautiful as well as dimensional. If you enjoy "Living Stereo" or "Surround Sound," I want you to imagine music coming from eleven different dimensional channels. Wouldn't you like to go to one of His concerts? Sit through one of His symphonies and you will understand the mysteries of math and the reason why scientists try to solve their problems and prove their theories with mathematical equations.

With God, you will find the sound of PURE TRUTH, depth, rhyme and reason, within His original Creations.

There will be those who refuse to see the deeper things of God, but I hope that is not you.

You are the one that God is trying to reach. I may not be the King of the Hill, or Lord of all that I survey, but I know the King of Kings and Lord of Lords, and that is what has made my life worth living, the good and the bad, the Light and the Shadow and the Truth that has formed my Reality.

Our conclusion has to be, that the SMALLEST ELEMENTS within the cellular level and DNA of Humans, dictates that there has to be "Intelligent Design" from a Creator.

Likewise, the universe was created by a force so small and powerful, that from the size of a pin point, God's Word exploded into the universe as we now know it, and it is held together by String Theory (an element so small, we can not see it.)

Only the mind of a Master Architect, Creator could have imagined and designed such a HUGE intelligent plan of so many dimensions. A plan so simple, yet so complex. A plan with details so small that it has confounded the wise of this earth.

And, yet He will divulge His Truth to us. Even His disciples were simple men, whom God choose to share and reveal His Eternal Drama and plan for the future.

If you have a problem with this book, please take it up with God.

If you like it, you may email your response directly to me personally; bishart@yahoo.com

EMAIL TO GOD

This is interesting....After a resent email that I sent, saying that email was like prayer, except with a different email address. "You just put down your thoughts, click a button and off it goes into cyber space". So I thought I would try it. I sent an email to God (www.god.org) This is what I got back:

"Suspected Recent Satellite Link Outage (Error 506)
The satellite link was operating properly up until the most recent web page request, but the last request could not be successfully sent across the satellite link to the DIRECWAY Network Operations Center. Possible causes for this include recent changes in weather conditions or equipment problems in the DIRECWAY Network Operations Center. **Retrying the web page may correct the problem."**

.... Or, maybe the email should have been sent to a different dimension in the space / time continuum.

And, I thought I had a direct way to God and His Network Operations Center!

I know what the problem was...I didn't send it in the "Name of Jesus".

Jan Douglas Bish

Original Paintings and Lithographs Available :

"*Lighthouse*" *by Jan Bish, in full color*
Original Painting on canvas 18x24,(framed)............*Page 28 $ 1,200.*

"*The New Jerusalem*" *by Jan Bish, 15x20*
Sheet Lithograph in full color...................................*Page 41 $ 75.00*

"*The Market Place*" *by Jan Bish, 24x30*
Original Painting on Canvas in full color...............*Page 67 $ 2,400.*

"*Revelation 12*" *in full color, 18x24*
Original Painting by Jan Bish in full color.............*Page 82 $ 1,200.*

Cover Painting by Jan Bish, 24x36
Original on Canvas "Alfama Fountain"...................................*$ 5,000.*

Send check or money order to:

Jan Bish, PO Box 986, Berryville, Arkansas 72616

Please check first on availability: bishart@yahoo.com

About the Author

Jan Douglas Bish is truly an artist and author, and actor.

He began his art career in Santa Barbara, California fifty years ago. Jan holds a U.S. Letters Patent on a collage process he originated and is represented by fine art galleries, book and art publishers internationally.

Jan lives in the Ozark Mountains during the summer months and mostly travels to exotic places internationally, during the winter season. He also likes to spend part of his winter in South Texas.

Bish plays a baritone ukulele as well as a six string and twelve string guitar. He has always had a love of good music, and theater.

After you have read one of Jan's books, you will know him better than any biography, or news release could ever describe.

"Light and Shadow" by Jan Bish is a book that explains Spiritual Truth through life experience, Biblical Scripture and Quantum Physics String Theory.

"Bequeath the Wind" by Jan Bish is a novel of adventure, love and intrigue through one year of his life. This is a must read for anyone who loves high adventure without getting down in the gutter with the bad guys.